Renewal in the
Seven Gifts
*Novena & Consecration
to the Holy Spirit*

Renewal in the Seven Gifts

*Novena & Consecration
to the Holy Spirit*

Denise Clare Oliver

Claritas Spiritual Theology

Spiritual Theology

Published 2023 by
Claritas Spiritual Theology®

London
claritas-st.com

ISBN: 978-1-8384876-2-1

Cover design by Denise Clare Oliver
Cover art – El Greco (1541-1614) Wikimedia Commons

Dedicated to the Holy Spirit,
Lord & Giver of Life,
Comforter & Guide

CONTENTS

Introduction

Renewal in the seven gifts through this Novena and Consecration to the Holy Spirit promotes a deeper awareness and a greater openness to the sanctifying action of the Holy Spirit through the operation of His sevenfold gift.

The charismatic renewal brought about a greater awareness of the Spirit's action through charismatic graces which are enumerated in 1 Cor. 12. The seven gifts of the Holy Spirit (Isa 11: 2-3) are often forgotten; yet it is these gifts which help us to soar in the spiritual life.

Both the charisms and the seven gifts are important; nevertheless, if we did not manifest any of the charisms in our whole lifetime, it would not affect our growth in holiness. The charisms are for the building up of the body of Christ; whereas the seven gifts of the Holy Spirit, received at baptism, are *necessary* for salvation.

All the baptised faithful have these dispositions (the gifts) within their soul if they are in a state of grace; but the Holy Spirit is the one Who puts these gifts into operation.

We can never decide when the Holy Spirit will work through His gifts, but we can certainly be better prepared for His action. Let us be ready for an outpouring of the Spirit through His sevenfold gift and promote a renewal in awareness of these most precious treasures. Let us begin with our own devotion to the Holy Spirit by praying this novena.

Christians continue to imitate the pattern of nine days of prayer before Pentecost. After Jesus ascended into heaven, the apostles and disciples returned to the upper room, and prayed together with the Blessed Virgin Mary for the coming of the Holy Spirit, as Jesus had instructed them to do, (Acts 1). After nine days of prayer, on the day of Pentecost, the apostles were filled with the Holy Spirit, (Acts 2).

The word novena is derived from the Latin word "novem" which means nine; a novena is a nine-day prayer which is said for a special intention. The intention might be for someone you love, it may be for yourself, or you might want to say a novena in thanksgiving for blessings or benefits already received. This novena is primarily intended to be prayed with the intention of asking the Lord for a special strengthening of His sevenfold gift, but it can also be prayed with a further intention in mind.

When praying a novena, it is important to keep our hearts and minds fixed on the Lord. It should not be something mechanical, but a real prayer from the heart. St Teresa of Avila says: "A prayer in which a person is not aware of whom he is speaking to, what he is asking, who it is who is asking and of whom, I do not call prayer however much the lips move." Let us speak to the Lord from the heart with attention, humility, and love!

Let us begin with our own devotion to the Holy Spirit by praying this novena and committing ourselves anew to being ready to follow His most holy inspirations. Through this nine-day novena may the Lord pour into our hearts an increase of His sevenfold gift each day and forevermore.

The prayer for each day of this Novena will be followed by one Our Father, one Hail Mary, and one Glory Be, followed by the Consecration prayer. The Consecration prayer is written on the pages of each day of this Novena so as not to interrupt the flow of your prayer.

OUR FATHER

Our Father, Who art in heaven,
Hallowed be Thy Name.
Thy kingdom come,
Thy Will be done,
on earth as it is in heaven.
Give us this day our daily bread.
And forgive us our trespasses,
as we forgive those who trespass against us.
And lead us not into temptation,
but deliver us from evil. Amen.

HAIL MARY

Hail Mary, full of grace,
The Lord is with thee.
Blessed art thou among women,
and blessed is the fruit of thy Womb, Jesus.
Holy Mary, Mother of God,
pray for us sinners,
now and at the hour of our death. Amen.

GLORY BE

Glory be to the Father,
and to the Son,
and to the Holy Spirit,
as it was in the beginning,
is now, and ever shall be,
world without end. Amen.

✛

CONSECRATION PRAYER

Come Holy Spirit, fill my heart with the fire of Your love, pour into my soul an increase of Your sevenfold gift. May I be forever inflamed by the power of Your love and always open to Your most holy inspirations.

O Holy Spirit, Divine Guest of my soul, work in me, guide me, and be forever my Comforter, my Advocate, and my Guide. May I never offend You, may I always be open to You, may I forever love You.

O Holy Spirit, enkindle within me an unending ardent love for You, so that I may never be separated from You, and when I draw my last breath, may it be inflamed with the fire of Your Infinite Divine Love. Amen.

DAY 1

THE SEVENFOLD GIFT

And there shall come forth a rod out of the root of Jesse, and a flower shall rise up out of his root. And the spirit of the Lord shall rest upon him: the spirit of wisdom, and of understanding, the spirit of counsel, and of fortitude, the spirit of knowledge, and of godliness. And he shall be filled with the spirit of the fear of the Lord.[1]

Isa 11:2-3

Come Holy Spirit, renew within me the fire of Your Love. Pour out Your Spirit upon me and strengthen within my soul Your sevenfold gift – the gift of wisdom, understanding, knowledge, counsel, piety, fortitude, and fear of the Lord.

May I remain open to Your most holy inspirations, so that each of these precious gifts continues to

---

[1] Scripture quotation taken from the Douay-Rheims 1899 American Edition; all other Scripture quotations contained in this work are taken from the Revised Standard Version Bible: Catholic Edition.

flourish within my soul.

May I never hinder the movement of Your promptings, and may I remain forever humble before You.

O Holy Spirit, carry me swiftly to the heights of holiness by way of Your sevenfold gift, so that inflamed with the fire of Your love, I may love You more tenderly, worship you more reverently, and forever sing praises to Father, Son, and Holy Spirit, world without end. Amen.

Our Father
Hail Mary
Glory Be

Consecration Prayer:

Come Holy Spirit, fill my heart with the fire of Your love, pour into my soul an increase of Your sevenfold gift. May I be forever inflamed by the power of Your love and always open to Your most holy inspirations.

O Holy Spirit, Divine Guest of my soul, work in me, guide me, and be forever my Comforter, my Advocate, and my Guide. May I never offend You, may I always be open to You, may I forever love You.

O Holy Spirit, enkindle within me an unending ardent love for You, so that I may never be separated from You, and when I draw my last breath, may it be inflamed with the fire of Your Infinite Divine Love. Amen.

DAY 2

THE GIFT OF FEAR

The fear of the Lord is the beginning of wisdom.
Ps 111:10 & Prov 9:10

Come Holy Spirit, fill my heart with a holy reverential fear of the Lord, cast out all servile fear, and renew within me that fear which stands in awe and reverence of God, so that I may turn away from all that is not holy and be filled with a firm hope and trust in your never-ending love and mercy.

O Holy Spirit, enkindle within my heart a perfect love which casts out all fear and which loves without end. May I be forever reverent and humble in Your sight. Amen.

Our Father
Hail Mary
Glory Be

Consecration Prayer

Come Holy Spirit, fill my heart with the fire of Your love, pour into my soul an increase of Your sevenfold gift. May I be forever inflamed by the power of Your love and always open to Your most holy inspirations.

O Holy Spirit, Divine Guest of my soul, work in me, guide me, and be forever my Comforter, my Advocate, and my Guide. May I never offend You, may I always be open to You, may I forever love You.

O Holy Spirit, enkindle within me an unending ardent love for You, so that I may never be separated from You, and when I draw my last breath, may it be inflamed with the fire of Your Infinite Divine Love. Amen.

DAY 3

THE GIFT OF FORTITUDE

When I am weak, then I am strong.
2 Cor 12:10

Come Holy Spirit, strengthen within me the gift of fortitude so that I may be forever faithful in all I do. May I have the strength to persevere in times of trial and temptation, and may I be always ready to stand up for the truth.

Pour out within my heart a renewed strength today and always, so that nothing may separate me from Your love.

May I hunger and thirst for justice, and may I always be willing to do all that you ask of me.

Finally, at the hour of death, may this precious gift give me strong wings to help carry me into that eternal bliss which awaits all those who remain faithful to the end. Amen.

Our Father
Hail Mary
Glory Be

Consecration Prayer:

Come Holy Spirit, fill my heart with the fire of Your love, pour into my soul an increase of Your sevenfold gift. May I be forever inflamed by the power of Your love and always open to Your most holy inspirations.

O Holy Spirit, Divine Guest of my soul, work in me, guide me, and be forever my Comforter, my Advocate, and my Guide. May I never offend You, may I always be open to You, may I forever love You.

O Holy Spirit, enkindle within me an unending ardent love for You, so that I may never be separated from You, and when I draw my last breath, may it be inflamed with the fire of Your Infinite Divine Love. Amen

DAY 4

THE GIFT OF PIETY

…you have received the spirit of sonship. When we cry 'Abba! Father!' it is the Spirit himself bearing witness with our spirit that we are children of God.
Rom. 8: 15-17

Come Holy Spirit, increase within me the gift of piety so that I may always look lovingly to my Heavenly Father as a child who rests in its father's arms.

Renew within me each day that filial love which melts the heart of God, and which fills me with confidence to run into the arms of the Father of mercies.

By way of this gift, may I see everyone as my brother or sister, whom I run to help in times of need.

When prayer is dry, fan within me the flame of Your love and pour out this most precious gift to give me fervour and renewed vigour in all my devotions.

With the outpouring of this gift, may I always be meek but strong, gentle but firm, trusting and trustworthy, and may I be forever a loving child who is pleasing to the Father. Amen.

Our Father
Hail Mary
Glory Be

Consecration Prayer:

Come Holy Spirit, fill my heart with the fire of Your love, pour into my soul an increase of Your sevenfold gift. May I be forever inflamed by the power of Your love and always open to Your most holy inspirations.

O Holy Spirit, Divine Guest of my soul, work in me, guide me, and be forever my Comforter, my Advocate, and my Guide. May I never offend You, may I always be open to You, may I forever love You.

O Holy Spirit, enkindle within me an unending ardent love for You, so that I may never be separated from You, and when I draw my last breath, may it be inflamed with the fire of Your Infinite Divine Love. Amen.

DAY 5

THE GIFT OF COUNSEL

*Thou dost guide me with thy counsel, and
afterward thou wilt receive me to glory.*
Ps 73:24

Come Holy Spirit, fill me with Your holy counsel
so that I may be forever faithful to your most Holy
Will. Come to my aid especially in times when I
have no time to think or act with prudence, or
when I cannot see the way forward.

Renew within me this most precious gift –
beautiful counsel of the Holy Spirit, come to my
aid.

Leave me not to my own ways, but teach me to be
docile to Your holy inspirations and to the people
You send to guide me. Lead me on the right path,
let me never go astray.

O good and precious Counselor and Guide, look
with favour upon me and guide me now and

always. Amen.

Our Father
Hail Mary
Glory Be

Consecration Prayer:

Come Holy Spirit, fill my heart with the fire of Your love, pour into my soul an increase of Your sevenfold gift. May I be forever inflamed by the power of Your love and always open to Your most holy inspirations.

O Holy Spirit, Divine Guest of my soul, work in me, guide me, and be forever my Comforter, my Advocate, and my Guide. May I never offend You, may I always be open to You, may I forever love You.

O Holy Spirit, enkindle within me an unending ardent love for You, so that I may never be separated from You, and when I draw my last breath, may it be inflamed with the fire of Your Infinite Divine Love. Amen.

DAY 6

THE GIFT OF KNOWLEDGE

Worthy art thou, our Lord and God, to receive glory and honor and power, for thou didst create all things, and by thy will they existed and were created.

Rev 4: 11

Come Holy Spirit, enlighten me with Your gift of knowledge so that I may see the vanity of passing things. Help me to turn away from all that is not holy and to fix my eyes on heavenly things.

Help me to lift my heart and mind to You and to give You all praise, honour, and glory, that I may be forever grateful for the Goodness of the Lord.

Through this gift, enable me to discern between good and evil, know truth from falsehood, and mourn all that offends you.

Finally, as a perfect fruit of this gift, may I be comforted by your Divine embrace both now and forever. Amen.

Our Father
Hail Mary
Glory Be

Consecration Prayer:

Come Holy Spirit, fill my heart with the fire of Your love, pour into my soul an increase of Your sevenfold gift. May I be forever inflamed by the power of Your love and always open to Your most holy inspirations.

O Holy Spirit, Divine Guest of my soul, work in me, guide me, and be forever my Comforter, my Advocate, and my Guide. May I never offend You, may I always be open to You, may I forever love You.

O Holy Spirit, enkindle within me an unending ardent love for You, so that I may never be separated from You, and when I draw my last breath, may it be inflamed with the fire of Your Infinite Divine Love. Amen.

DAY 7

THE GIFT OF UNDERSTANDING

*Then He opened their minds
to understand the scriptures.*
Luke 24:45

Come Holy Spirit, strengthen within me Your gift of understanding, and give me a deep penetration into the hidden meaning of Your Divine truths, that I may receive new lights.

Cleanse my mind of all erroneous thinking, ideas, or images, which I may have formed about God. Holy Spirit, Advocate, and welcome Guest of my soul, remove from me all dullness of mind.

Give me clarity so that I may see my own littleness and weakness in comparison to the awesome splendour and grandeur of God.

Finally, may this precious gift perfect my faith and make me pure in spirit, so that I can always draw closer to the Most Holy Trinity, One God and

Three Persons, Who reign without end. Amen.

Our Father
Hail Mary
Glory Be

Consecration Prayer:

Come Holy Spirit, fill my heart with the fire of Your love, pour into my soul an increase of Your sevenfold gift. May I be forever inflamed by the power of Your love and always open to Your most holy inspirations.

O Holy Spirit, Divine Guest of my soul, work in me, guide me, and be forever my Comforter, my Advocate, and my Guide. May I never offend You, may I always be open to You, may I forever love You.

O Holy Spirit, enkindle within me an unending ardent love for You, so that I may never be separated from You, and when I draw my last breath, may it be inflamed with the fire of Your Infinite Divine Love. Amen.

DAY 8

THE GIFT OF WISDOM

O taste and see that the LORD is good!
Ps 34:8

Come Holy Spirit, enkindle within me the fire of Your love, that through the gift of wisdom, I may see all things through God's eyes. And with this Divine glance, may I see the wonder and mystery of God's most Holy Will. Fill me with the fire of Your love and with perfect charity through this most precious gift.

Order all my disordered affections, so that I may have peace within my soul and be at peace with all those whom I meet.

Through this gift may I taste and see that the Lord is good, and delight in His irresistible tender love which ravishes the soul.

Finally, may I always love God above all things, and one day reach that eternal bliss where the heart will rest in eternal delight and peace without end. Amen.

Our Father
Hail Mary
Glory Be

Consecration Prayer:

Come Holy Spirit, fill my heart with the fire of Your love, pour into my soul an increase of Your sevenfold gift. May I be forever inflamed by the power of Your love and always open to Your most holy inspirations.

O Holy Spirit, Divine Guest of my soul, work in me, guide me, and be forever my Comforter, my Advocate, and my Guide. May I never offend You, may I always be open to You, may I forever love You.

O Holy Spirit, enkindle within me an unending ardent love for You, so that I may never be separated from You, and when I draw my last breath, may it be inflamed with the fire of Your Infinite Divine Love. Amen

THE BEATITUDES: PERFECT FRUITS

Blessed are the poor in spirit, for theirs is the kingdom of heaven. Blessed are those who mourn, for they shall be comforted. Blessed are the meek, for they shall inherit the earth. Blessed are those who hunger and thirst for righteousness, for they shall be satisfied. Blessed are the merciful, for they shall obtain mercy. Blessed are the pure in heart, for they shall see God. Blessed are the peacemakers, for they shall be called sons of God. Blessed are those who are persecuted for righteousness' sake, for theirs is the kingdom of heaven.
Mt 5:3-10

Come Holy Spirit, consume my life with the fire of Your love. May I be so moved by Your heavenly inspirations, that the beatitudes which flow from the gifts always shine brightly in my life.

By way of the gift of fear, may I remain poor in spirit; through the gift of piety, may I be always meek; by way of the gift of fortitude, may I always hunger and thirst after justice; may the gift of knowledge help me to mourn all that offends You; with the gift of understanding, make me pure of spirit; and fill me with unending peace through the gift of wisdom, the apex of all Your gifts.

May all these most perfect fruits radiate the light of Your wisdom and the warmth of Your love and may I go forth to proclaim Your infinite goodness, and to give all glory to the Most Holy Trinity forever and ever. Amen.

Our Father
Hail Mary
Glory Be

Final Consecration Prayer:

Come Holy Spirit, fill my heart with the fire of Your love, pour into my soul an increase of Your sevenfold gift. May I be forever inflamed by the power of Your love and always open to Your most holy inspirations.

O Holy Spirit, Divine Guest of my soul, work in me, guide me, and be forever my Comforter, my Advocate, and my Guide. May I never offend You, may I always be open to You, may I forever love You.

O Holy Spirit, enkindle within me an unending ardent love for You, so that I may never be separated from You, and when I draw my last breath, may it be inflamed with the fire of Your Infinite Divine Love.

Renewed in fervour by the power of your grace, my heart is an ever open vessel which awaits an outpouring of your most holy inspirations. I desire to follow Your promptings with a heart that is always focused on doing Your most holy Will.

O Holy Spirit! Sweet welcome Guest of my soul, please fill me with your grace and strengthen within me your sevenfold gift today and each day, so that when I finally draw my last breath your familiar presence will guide me into that eternal embrace which is without end. Amen.

Printed in Great Britain
by Amazon